The Birthmark of the Believer

Joshua Rhoades

Published by Joshua Paul Rhoades, 2024.

While every precaution has been taken in the preparation of this book, the publisher assumes no responsibility for errors or omissions, or for damages resulting from the use of the information contained herein.

THE BIRTHMARK OF THE BELIEVER

First edition. October 12, 2024.

ISBN: 979-8224475995

Written by Joshua Rhoades.

Also by Joshua Rhoades

Courage Under Fire: David's Stand On The Battlefield
Jonah's Journey: Voices Of Redemption And Lessons In Obedience
The Furnace Of Faith: 12 Principles From The Heat Of Faith
Whispers of Hope: Inspiring Stories of Men's Prayers In Scripture
Frontier Legends: The Oregon Dream
Elijah: A Beacon Of Boldness
HOOK, LINE & SAVIOUR - Faith Reflections from Fishing
Driven By Faith: Motor Racing Inspired Christian Life
30 Day Devotional - Bold and Strong- Coffee Devotions for a Courageous Christian Walk
Authentic Christianity: The Heart of Old Time Religion
Consider The Ant - God's Tiny Preachers
Flee Fornication: The Plea For Purity
Renewed Hope- How to Find Encouragement in God
Sounding The Call - The Voice of Conviction
The Altar - Where Heaven Meets Earth
The Bible's Battlefields- Timeless Lessons from Ancient Wars
The Sacred Art of Silence - How Silence Speaks in Scripture
Under Fire- The Sanctity of the Traditional Biblical Home
Who Is on the Lord's Side? A Call to Righteousness
What Is Truth? - From Skepticism to Submission
First and Goal- Faith and Football Fundamentals
From Dugout to Devotion- Spiritual Lessons from Baseball
Par for the Course- Faith and Fairways
The Believer's Pace- Tools for Running Life's Marathon
The Immutable Fortress- Security in God's Unchanging Nature
Biblical Bravery
Deer Stands and Devotions: A Hunter's Walk with God

Jesus Knows- Our Hearts, Our Responsibility
Restoration - Setting The Bone
Spiritual 911- God's Word for Life's Emergency's
The Freedom of Forgiveness
The Jezebel Effect - Ancient Manipulations Modern Lessons
The Shout That Stopped The Saviour
The Time Machine Chronicles: Old Testament Characters
Anchored In Truth Exploring The Depths of Psalm 119
Biblical Counsel on Anger
Proverbs' Portraits The Men God Mentions
Stumbling in the Dark - The Dangers of Alcohol
Guarding the Wicket Protecting Your Faith and Game
The Champion's Faith - Wrestling and Achieving Spiritual Victory
Scriptural Commands for Modern Times Living God's Word Today Volume 1
Scriptural Commands for Modern Times Living God's Word Today Volume 2
Scriptural Commands for Modern Times Living God's Word TodayVolume3
The Greatest Gift
A Christmas Journey of Faith
Daughter Of The King: Embracing Your Identity In Christ
Determination and Dedication Building Strong Faith As A Young Man
Walking Through Walls God's Power to Part the Storms of Life
David's Song Of Deliverance Praising God Through Every Storm
From Weakness to Warrior: Gideon's Transformation
Why Did Jesus Weep?
Living For God The Call To Be A Living Sacrifice
My Mind Is In A Fog What Do I Do?
Turning The Page Written By Grace
The Calling and Greatness of John the Baptist
For Such a Time Esther's Courageous Stand
From Brokenness To Beauty Written By The Pen of Grace
The Ultimate Guide to Massive Action- From Plans to Reality
A Heart Of Conviction
Serving In The Shadows
Repentance Revealed The Road Back To God
The Chief Sinner Meets The Chief Saviour Reflections On I Timothy 1:15

Answer The Call - 31 Days of Biblical Action
The Birthmark of the Believer

"The Birthmark of the Believer" is a powerful and uplifting exploration of what it means to carry the unique mark of faith in Christ. Just like a birthmark makes a person stand out physically, our faith sets us apart spiritually. This book looks into the challenges and beauty of living as a follower of Jesus in a world that often doesn't understand or accept faith. It encourages believers to embrace their identity in Christ with confidence, knowing that they are chosen, loved, and called for a divine purpose. Whether you've been walking with God for years or are just beginning your spiritual journey, this book offers encouragement and guidance to help you live boldly for Christ. It reminds us that, no matter the struggles we face or the judgments we encounter, our birthmark of faith is a beautiful reminder of God's love and grace at work in our lives. You are not just another face in the crowd—you are marked by the love of Christ, and this mark defines who you are and who you are becoming.

Introduction

Welcome to "The Birthmark of the Believer," a journey into understanding the beautiful and unique mark that sets Christians apart. Just like a birthmark is personal and distinguishing, so is the faith we carry as believers. As children of God, we each have a spiritual birthmark, an identity that defines who we are in Christ. This mark, invisible to the eye but visible in our actions, reflects the grace, love, and truth that God has placed in our hearts. Throughout this book, we'll explore what it means to carry this birthmark as we walk through the ups and downs of life. We'll talk about how our faith can shape us, how our relationship with God transforms us, and how the world sees us as followers of Jesus. Life as a believer isn't always easy. There will be challenges, doubts, and moments when standing firm in our faith feels heavy. Just like how a birthmark might bring self-consciousness or make us feel different, being a believer in a world that often rejects or misunderstands our faith can make us feel out of place. But this birthmark we carry is not something to be hidden or ashamed of. It's something that sets us apart in the most beautiful way. Our faith marks us as beloved children of God with a purpose and calling that is far greater than we often realize. As we dive deeper into what it means to live as a marked believer, we'll look at the struggles and triumphs that come with it. We'll talk about how God refines us through trials, how He heals us from the wounds of our past, and how He continually molds us into the people He has called us to be. The process of growing in faith, of becoming more like Jesus, can sometimes be uncomfortable, but it's in this refining process that we become the person God designed us to be. Throughout the pages of this book, I hope you'll find encouragement, strength, and hope. Whether you've been walking with God for years or you're just beginning your journey of faith, remember that your spiritual birthmark is a sign of God's presence in your life. It's a reminder that you are set apart, loved, and chosen by Him. The world may not always understand or appreciate the mark you carry, but rest assured that it is precious in God's eyes. This birthmark of faith is a gift, and it is something that will grow and flourish as you walk closely with your Savior. So, as we embark on this journey together, I invite you to embrace your spiritual birthmark. Let it be a source of strength and confidence as you navigate the joys and challenges of life as a believer. My prayer is that through these words, you will be reminded of your incredible worth in Christ, and that you will walk boldly in the knowledge that you are marked by His love and grace.

Chapter 1 - Position

Each Christian has a unique position in life, just like a birthmark has a specific place on the body that cannot be moved or changed easily. When we think about how a birthmark is a part of someone's identity, we can start to understand that our position in life, our role, and where God has placed us are just as important in defining who we are in Christ. God has set each one of us in a specific place for a reason, and it is all part of His greater plan. Whether we are given a role that is visible to many people, like being a teacher, a pastor, or a leader, or we are in a more hidden role, such as helping others quietly, working in the background, or serving our family, every position is valuable and purposeful. Sometimes, we may feel like our role or position is small, insignificant, or not as important as someone else's, but that's simply not true. Just like every part of the human body is necessary for it to work properly, every Christian is needed to make the body of Christ function as it should. Imagine a body missing a part, even a small one like a finger or a toe. It wouldn't work as well, right? The same goes for the church and the Christian life. Every believer is placed where they are for a reason, and without each person doing their part, something is missing.

We often struggle with comparing ourselves to others. We might think, "I wish I could do what they are doing," or "Why am I stuck in this position while others are doing something that seems more important or exciting?" But we must remember that God's plan is far greater than what we can see in the moment. He has a specific purpose for placing us where we are, and that purpose might not be fully clear right now, but it is part of a bigger picture that we may not yet understand. Think about a puzzle. Each piece is important, and even though a single piece might not make sense on its own, once it's connected to the others, the entire image becomes clear. Our position in life is like one of those puzzle pieces. It might seem small or insignificant when we look at it alone, but it plays a crucial part in the overall picture of what God is doing in the world.

In 1 Corinthians 12:18, the Bible says, "But now hath God set the members every one of them in the body, as it hath pleased him." This means that God, in His wisdom and goodness, has placed each one of us in the body of Christ exactly where He wants us to be. It brings God pleasure to put us in the right spot, just as a master artist places each stroke of paint exactly where it belongs to create a masterpiece. It might be tempting to question God's decisions or wonder why we are where we are, but trusting in His plan is key to finding peace and contentment. It's not about being in the spotlight or doing the most visible work; it's about being faithful in whatever position God has given us. Some of the most important parts of a machine are hidden inside, never seen by anyone, but without them, the machine would break down. The same is true for us as Christians. Even if our role seems small or unnoticed, it is essential to God's plan, and it is making a difference, even if we don't see it right away.

Let's think about the life of Jesus. During His time on earth, He didn't seek out the positions that brought the most attention or praise. He often worked quietly, serving others in humble ways. He washed His disciples' feet, spent time with people who were overlooked by society, and cared for the sick and the poor. Jesus showed us that true greatness in God's kingdom is not about being the most powerful or the most famous, but about serving others with love and humility. In the same way, our position in life might not always be glamorous or recognized by the world, but if we are serving God and others faithfully, we are doing exactly what He has called us to do.

Sometimes, we might face challenges or hardships in our position. It can be hard to stay positive and motivated when things aren't going the way we hoped, or when it feels like our efforts aren't making a difference. But during these times, we can find strength in knowing that God sees our efforts and is with us every step of the way. He doesn't place us in difficult situations without giving us the grace and strength to handle them. Just as a plant needs sunlight, water, and time to grow, we need to trust that God is providing what we need to grow in our position. And just like a plant eventually bears fruit, our faithfulness will bear fruit in God's timing.

One of the most beautiful things about being part of the body of Christ is that we are not alone. Just as a birthmark is part of a person's body, we are part of something much bigger than ourselves. We are part of a family of believers, all working together for God's kingdom. Each of us has a role to play, and when we work together, amazing things can happen. We can support each other, encourage each other, and lift each other up when times get tough. When we see someone struggling, we can remind them of the importance of their position and help them see that they are making a difference. And when we are struggling, we can rely on others to remind us of the same.

It's also important to remember that our position in life might change over time. Just because God has placed us in one spot now doesn't mean we will always be in that same position. Sometimes, God moves us to new places or gives us new responsibilities as we grow and develop. But wherever we are, we can trust that God has a purpose for us in that place. Whether we are young or old, experienced or just starting out, God can use us in powerful ways if we are willing to serve Him with our whole heart.

One example of this can be seen in the life of the Apostle Paul. Before his conversion, Paul was in a position of authority, but he was using that position to persecute Christians. However, after encountering Jesus on the road to Damascus, Paul's position changed completely. God placed him in a new role, where he became one of the most influential leaders in the early church. Paul's story shows us that no matter where we start, God can change our position and use us for His glory. It also shows that God is always at work, even when we don't realize it.

In conclusion, our position in life, whether it is public or private, big or small, is important to God. He has placed us where we are for a reason, and we can trust that His plan is good. We don't need to compare ourselves to others or wish we were in a different place because God knows what is best for us and for His kingdom. Our job is to be faithful in the position we have been given, serving others with love and humility, just as Jesus did. We are part of something much bigger than ourselves, and each of us plays an important role in the body of Christ. Whether we are in a season of growth or a season of waiting, we can trust that God is with us, guiding us, and using us for His purposes. So, let's embrace our position, serve faithfully, and trust that God is at work, even when we can't see it. Just like a birthmark is part of someone's identity, our position is part of our identity in Christ, and that makes it valuable and meaningful.

Chapter 2 – Presentation

Just like birthmarks come in different colors, shapes, and sizes, Christians are unique in how they show their faith and love for God to the world. No two people are exactly alike, and the way we present Christ through our lives is as diverse as the different forms that birthmarks take. Each of us has a special way of reflecting God's light. It might be through the way we treat others, the words we speak, or the way we serve and help those in need. Just as some birthmarks are more visible while others are hidden, some people express their faith openly and boldly, while others do it more quietly and subtly. But no matter how we present our faith, it's important to remember that we are all called to be the light of the world, as Jesus tells us in Matthew 5:14: "Ye are the light of the world. A city that is set on a hill cannot be hid." This means that, as Christians, we are meant to stand out, not in a way that draws attention to ourselves but in a way that points others to Jesus. Just like a city on a hill that can be seen from miles away, our lives should reflect God's love and truth for all to see. Whether we are in school, at work, with friends, or with family, people should be able to see something different about us, something that shows we belong to Christ.

Sometimes, we might feel like the way we present our faith isn't good enough or that it doesn't measure up to how others express theirs. We might look at someone who speaks confidently about Jesus in front of large crowds or someone who seems to always know the right thing to say and think, "I could never do that." But the truth is, God has given each of us different gifts and ways to show His light, and all of them are important. Just like a birthmark is part of a person's unique identity, the way we present our faith is part of who we are in Christ. Some people are gifted with the ability to preach or teach, while others are gifted in showing kindness, serving quietly, or being a listening ear to someone who needs it. The important thing is not how we present our faith compared to others, but that we are faithful in doing it in the way God has called us to.

One of the most amazing things about being a Christian is that God uses our personalities, our strengths, and even our weaknesses to show His light to the world. He doesn't ask us to be someone we're not; He simply asks us to be who He created us to be and to let His love shine through us. Just as a birthmark can't be changed or moved, the way we are meant to present Christ is a natural part of who we are. God designed each of us with a purpose, and He knows how our unique way of living out our faith can impact the people around us. Sometimes, the way we present Christ might be through big actions, like helping someone in need or standing up for what's right, but often, it's in the small, everyday things: being kind to someone who is having a hard day, offering a smile, or simply being there for a friend. These little acts of love and kindness are like rays of light that show others who God is and how much He loves them.

It's also important to remember that we don't have to be perfect in how we present Christ. Just as a birthmark might have imperfections or look different from what we expect, we might feel like we don't always get it right when it comes to living out our faith. We might say the wrong thing, make mistakes, or feel like we're not doing enough. But God's light shines through us, even in our imperfections. In fact, it's often through our struggles and weaknesses that others can see the power of God at work in our lives. When we are honest about our challenges and show how God helps us through them, it can be a powerful testimony to others about His grace and love. We don't have to have it all together to present Christ to the world. We just have to be willing to let God use us as we are, trusting that He will shine His light through us.

Another thing to consider is that just as birthmarks are permanent, our role as the light of the world is something that stays with us. It's not something we turn on and off depending on where we are or who we're with. Being a light means that every part of our life is meant to reflect Jesus. Whether we are at home, at school, at work, or with friends, we are called to let our light shine. This doesn't mean we have to be constantly talking about our faith or trying to prove something. It simply means that we live in a way that shows others the love, kindness, and truth of God. People should be able to see the difference in how we live our lives because of our relationship with Jesus.

Sometimes, being the light of the world isn't easy. We live in a world that often rejects God's truth and can make it difficult to stand out for our faith. There may be times when we feel pressured to hide our light or blend in with everyone else. But Jesus tells us that a city on a hill cannot be hidden. In the same way, we shouldn't hide our faith, even when it's hard. God has called us to be His representatives in the world, and He gives us the strength and courage to do that, even when it's challenging. When we feel like the world is pushing back against our faith, we can remember that God is with us and that His light is stronger than the darkness.

One of the most beautiful things about being the light of the world is that we don't do it alone. Just as a birthmark is part of a person's body, we are part of the body of Christ, and we are all in this together. When we come together with other believers, our lights shine even brighter. We can encourage each other, support each other, and help each other grow in our faith. Just like how different parts of the body work together to make the whole body function, we all have different roles to play in showing Christ to the world. When we work together, we can have an even greater impact.

In Matthew 5:14, Jesus reminds us that we are the light of the world, and this is an incredible responsibility but also an incredible privilege. We have the opportunity to make a difference in the world by simply being who God has called us to be. We don't have to be someone else or try to fit into a mold. God has made each of us unique, and He uses our distinct personalities and ways of expressing faith to reach people in ways that only we can. Just as birthmarks are presented in different ways, our lives present the light of Christ in different ways, and that is something to celebrate. When we embrace who we are in Christ and let His light shine through us, we can bring hope, love, and truth to a world that desperately needs it.

Ultimately, being the light of the world is about reflecting the love of Jesus to others. Just as birthmarks are a visible part of someone's identity, our faith should be a visible part of who we are. It should be something that others can see in the way we live our lives, in the way we treat people, and in the choices we make. We are not called to hide our faith or keep it to ourselves. We are called to let it shine brightly so that others can see the goodness of God. And when they see that light in us, they will be drawn to the source of that light—Jesus.

In conclusion, just as birthmarks are presented in different colors and forms, Christians present the light of Christ through their distinct personalities and expressions of faith. We don't all have to look the same or act the same to be faithful in showing the world who Jesus is. God has given each of us a unique way of expressing His love, and when we embrace that, we can have a powerful impact on those around us. Whether through bold actions or quiet kindness, whether in public or private, we are all called to be the light of the world. And just as a city on a hill cannot be hidden, neither should our faith. Let's live in a way that reflects the love and truth of Christ, shining His light for all to see.

Chapter 3 – Pattern

Just like the unique patterns that make up birthmarks on a person's body, each Christian's life is shaped by a distinctive journey of faith. No two people's paths are exactly the same, and each person's Christian walk forms a pattern that reflects the unique ways God is working in their life. Think about how every birthmark is different — some are small, some are large, some are round, some are uneven, and no two are ever identical. In the same way, each Christian's relationship with God is unique and personal. Your experiences, challenges, and the ways you grow in your faith are all part of a pattern that God is carefully crafting. As Ephesians 2:10 tells us, "For we are his workmanship, created in Christ Jesus unto good works, which God hath before ordained that we should walk in them." This means that every part of our lives, every moment, every decision, every triumph, and every failure is woven into a beautiful pattern that God Himself has designed. He is the master artist, and we are His creation, made for a purpose that He had in mind long before we were even born.

Sometimes, when we look at our lives, it can be hard to see the pattern. We might feel like things are messy, unclear, or confusing, much like a birthmark that doesn't have a clear shape. We might wonder why certain things are happening to us or why our lives don't look like the lives of other Christians we know. It's easy to compare our journey with others and think that we're not doing as well as they are, or that we're not growing in our faith the way we should. But just like a birthmark's shape is a natural part of a person's body, the pattern of our lives is a natural part of God's plan for us. We don't have to try to force our lives to look like someone else's because God has designed a unique journey for each of us. What might seem like a confusing or difficult season in our life is actually a crucial part of the pattern that God is weaving. Every experience, both good and bad, is used by God to shape us into the people He created us to be.

In a birthmark, you can see different lines, shapes, and colors that come together to form something that is one-of-a-kind. In our Christian lives, the different "lines" are the experiences we go through — the moments of joy, the times of struggle, the lessons we learn, and the relationships we build. Each of these experiences adds to the pattern, and over time, they begin to show the bigger picture of what God is doing in our lives. We may not always understand why certain things happen to us or why God leads us down certain paths, but we can trust that He is using every part of our journey to create something beautiful. Just like an artist who starts with a blank canvas and carefully adds strokes of paint, God is adding moments, decisions, and experiences to the canvas of our lives, and each one is intentional. Nothing in our lives is wasted, even the difficult times. In fact, it is often during the hardest moments that God does some of His most important work in shaping our pattern.

When we face challenges or obstacles, it can feel like the pattern of our life is being torn apart or messed up. We might think that we've taken a wrong turn or that God has forgotten about us. But the truth is, God is still in control, even when things don't make sense to us. He sees the entire picture, while we only see a small part. What looks like a mistake or a detour to us is actually a part of God's plan to shape us into who we are meant to be. Just like a birthmark might have an unexpected shape or appear in an unexpected place, the twists and turns of our lives are often surprising, but they are never outside of God's control. He is always working behind the scenes, guiding us and molding us into His image.

One of the most comforting things about being a Christian is knowing that we are not in this journey alone. God is with us every step of the way, and He is the one who is shaping the pattern of our lives. We don't have to figure it all out on our own or worry about whether we are doing enough. God has already ordained the good works that we should walk in, as Ephesians 2:10 says. He has already planned out the path for us, and our job is simply to trust Him and follow where He leads. Sometimes that path will be clear and easy to walk, and other times it will be difficult and filled with obstacles. But no matter what, we can trust that God is using every step we take to create a pattern that reflects His glory.

It's also important to remember that the pattern of our lives is not just about us. As Christians, we are called to reflect the light of Christ to the world, and the way we live our lives is a testimony to God's goodness and grace. Just like how a birthmark is a visible part of someone's appearance, the pattern of our lives is a visible reflection of God's handiwork. When people see the way we live — how we respond to challenges, how we treat others, and how we pursue God — they are seeing the pattern that God is creating in us. Our lives are meant to point others to Jesus, and the unique pattern of our journey can be a powerful testimony to those around us. Even the parts of our lives that seem messy or broken can be used by God to show others His love and faithfulness. In fact, it is often through our weaknesses and struggles that God's strength is most clearly seen.

The pattern of our Christian walk is not something that we can fully understand while we are still on this earth. Just like how a birthmark can look different depending on the angle or lighting, our lives can seem confusing or unclear at times. But one day, when we are with God in eternity, we will be able to see the full picture. We will be able to look back and see how every moment, every decision, and every experience was part of the beautiful pattern that God was weaving. In that moment, we will understand how even the hard times and the struggles were used by God to shape us and make us more like Christ.

As we continue on this journey of faith, it's important to remember that the pattern of our lives is a work in progress. We are not finished yet, and God is still working in us and through us. There will be times when we feel like we are making progress, and there will be times when we feel stuck or lost. But no matter what, God is still at work, and He is still shaping the pattern of our lives. We can trust that He knows what He is doing, even when we don't. He is the master artist, and we are His masterpiece. Every line, every color, and every shape is carefully chosen by Him, and the final result will be more beautiful than we can imagine.

In conclusion, just as the shape of a birthmark is unique to each person, the pattern of our Christian walk is unique to each of us. God is shaping our lives in ways that reflect His glory and His purpose for us. We may not always understand the pattern while we are in the middle of it, but we can trust that God is in control and that He is using every part of our journey to create something beautiful. As Ephesians 2:10 reminds us, we are His workmanship, created in Christ Jesus for good works that God has already prepared for us. Our job is to trust Him, follow Him, and let Him shape the pattern of our lives in a way that reflects His love and grace to the world. No matter what twists and turns our journey takes, we can have confidence that God is with us, guiding us, and working in us to create a pattern that will ultimately glorify Him. So let's embrace the unique pattern that God is creating in our lives and trust that He is using every moment to shape us into the people He has called us to be.

Chapter 4 – Proportion

Just like the size of a birthmark can vary greatly, from tiny to large, the influence each Christian has in this world also varies. Some people are called to lead many, to speak to large crowds, or to have a significant impact in the public eye. Others are called to smaller, more private roles, influencing only a few people closely around them. Yet, no matter the size of the platform or the number of people we reach, every role and every influence is equally valuable in the eyes of God. Just as a small birthmark is still part of a person's identity and contributes to their unique appearance, a believer with a smaller circle of influence is just as important in God's plan as someone who may have a wider reach. Jesus reminds us in Luke 12:48, "But he that knew not, and did commit things worthy of stripes, shall be beaten with few stripes. For unto whomsoever much is given, of him shall be much required: and to whom men have committed much, of him they will ask the more." and this speaks directly to the idea that God gives each of us different responsibilities according to His purpose for our lives. If we are given much, God expects us to use it for His glory. If we are given less, He still calls us to be faithful with what we have. The amount doesn't matter to God; it's the faithfulness that counts.

Often, we might feel like the scope of our influence is too small or insignificant. It's easy to look at others who have larger platforms — maybe someone who speaks at big events, someone who writes books that touch millions of lives, or someone who is well-known for their faith — and think that our contribution doesn't matter as much. But just like a small birthmark still has its place on the body, each Christian's role has its place in the Kingdom of God. The truth is, God has designed each of us uniquely, and He places us in exactly the right place to influence the people we are meant to reach. No one else can do what we do in the exact way we do it. Whether we are called to serve in front of many or behind the scenes, whether our actions are noticed by a few or by thousands, it is all valuable in the eyes of the Lord. In fact, some of the most important and impactful things we can do for the Kingdom of God might go completely unnoticed by the world. That doesn't make them any less significant. What matters most is not the size of our influence but the heart with which we carry out the tasks God has given us.

Consider how a small, seemingly insignificant action can have a ripple effect. Just as a birthmark, no matter its size, is a permanent part of someone's appearance, the small acts of kindness, encouragement, and faith that we offer to those around us can have lasting effects that we may never fully understand. A kind word spoken in a moment of need, a prayer for a friend who is struggling, or simply living a life that reflects the love of Christ can influence others in ways that reach far beyond what we can see. It's possible that the people we influence will go on to impact others, creating a chain reaction of faith and love that spreads further than we could have imagined. This is why it's so important not to underestimate the value of what we do, no matter how small it may seem at the time. We may never know the full extent of our influence until we are in Heaven, but we can trust that God is using every part of our lives for His purposes.

On the other hand, some Christians are given larger platforms and more visible roles in the Kingdom. These people may have more resources, more opportunities, or more people looking to them for guidance. With that greater influence comes greater responsibility, as Jesus points out in Luke 12:48. Those who are entrusted with much are expected to use it wisely and for God's glory. It can be easy to get caught up in the idea of influence and power, but God reminds us that with great influence comes a great responsibility to serve others humbly and faithfully. Just as a large birthmark might be more noticeable but doesn't change the person's worth compared to someone with a smaller birthmark, those with larger platforms are not more valuable in God's eyes than those with smaller ones. The key is that everyone, no matter the size of their influence, is called to serve with the same heart of obedience, humility, and love.

It's also important to remember that the scope of our influence can change throughout our lives. Just like a birthmark can grow or fade over time, the ways in which we impact others might grow or shift as we move through different seasons of life. There may be times when God calls us to reach a wider audience, and there may be other times when He calls us to focus on just a few people. Sometimes, we might be called to influence the same group of people for many years, while at other times, God might move us into new situations with new opportunities to reach others. Wherever He places us, our job is to be faithful and to trust that He is using us exactly where we need to be. We don't have to strive for a bigger platform or feel discouraged if our circle of influence seems small. God knows what He is doing, and His timing and purposes are always perfect.

Another aspect of influence is understanding that it's not always about how many people we reach but how deeply we reach them. Sometimes, the most impactful influence we can have is on just one person. Think about how Jesus, while He preached to crowds, also took the time to build deep, personal relationships with individuals. He invested in His disciples, teaching them, guiding them, and showing them love and grace. Those twelve men went on to change the world with the message of the Gospel. In the same way, we might be called to pour into the lives of just a few people, but the depth of that investment can make a profound difference. Whether we are teaching our children, encouraging a friend, or mentoring someone in their faith, those small, focused acts of influence can have eternal significance.

As Christians, we must also be aware that our influence is not just about what we say but also about how we live. People are watching us, whether we realize it or not, and our actions often speak louder than words. Just as a birthmark is a visible part of a person's body, our faith should be a visible part of our lives. The way we handle difficult situations, how we treat others, how we respond to challenges, and how we demonstrate love and grace in our everyday lives all reflect the light of Christ to those around us. We don't have to have all the answers or be perfect, but we do need to live in a way that points others to Jesus. Sometimes, the most powerful influence we can have is simply living out our faith with integrity and love, showing others through our actions what it means to follow Christ.

In the end, the size of our platform or the number of people we reach is not what matters most. What matters is that we are faithful stewards of the influence God has given us. Whether we are called to reach many or a few, God looks at our hearts and our willingness to serve Him. We don't need to worry about comparing ourselves to others or feeling like we're not doing enough. God knows exactly what He has entrusted to us, and He knows how He wants to use us for His purposes. Our job is to be faithful, to trust in His plan, and to do the work

He has called us to do with a heart full of love and obedience. Whether our influence seems big or small, it all matters to God, and it all contributes to His Kingdom in ways that we may not fully understand.

In conclusion, just as the size of a birthmark varies from person to person, the scope of each believer's influence is different. Some are called to large platforms, others to small circles, but both are equally valuable in the eyes of God. No matter the size of our influence, we are called to be faithful stewards of what God has given us, knowing that every action, no matter how small, can have a lasting impact for His Kingdom. We are reminded in Luke 12:48 that "unto whomsoever much is given, of him shall be much required:" and this teaches us that with great influence comes great responsibility. But even those with smaller circles of influence are just as important in God's plan. The size of our platform does not determine our worth or the value of our work for the Kingdom. God calls each of us to serve in the ways He has prepared for us, and He uses our unique gifts and opportunities to spread His love and truth to the world. Whether our influence is large or small, it is part of God's greater plan, and when we are faithful to His calling, we can trust that He will use us to make a difference, one life at a time.

Chapter 5 – Purpose

Just as every birthmark is unique, serving different purposes, so too are the lives of Christians shaped with distinct gifts, callings, and purposes in God's Kingdom. Think about how each birthmark is part of someone's identity—its shape, size, and placement are never the same from person to person, and it serves a purpose, whether medical or simply as a characteristic that makes each individual distinct. In the same way, God has designed each believer to play a special role in His grand plan, and no two people are exactly alike in what they are called to do. Some people are given the gift of teaching, some the gift of encouragement, others the gift of serving, and some are called to lead, while others are called to support from the background. Just as every birthmark is important to the person it belongs to, every calling and gift is important to God. Romans 12:6 reminds us that "Having then gifts differing according to the grace that is given to us, whether prophecy, let us prophesy according to the proportion of faith." This means that God has given each of us gifts that fit us perfectly, and it's according to His grace that we are able to use those gifts in ways that impact others and glorify Him.

Often, we may feel like our gifts aren't as important or visible as someone else's. We might look at people who seem to be more talented or gifted and think that our role in God's Kingdom doesn't matter as much. But this is far from the truth. Just as every part of the human body serves a unique function, every believer has a purpose that is vital to the whole body of Christ. Consider how your hand has a different function than your eye, and yet, both are essential to the body's overall well-being. In the same way, your gifts, no matter how small or large they may seem, are crucial to God's plan. Some are called to use their gifts in more visible ways, such as preaching or leading large groups, while others are called to minister quietly, perhaps through prayer, encouragement, or acts of service that go unseen by most. But the beauty of God's design is that He values all roles equally, and each one is important in its own right. Whether we are prophesying to a crowd or showing love to someone who feels forgotten, we are fulfilling God's purpose for our lives.

The purpose God has for us is not something we must figure out on our own. He has already placed it within us, woven into the fabric of who we are, just as a birthmark is a natural part of a person's body. When we draw closer to God and seek His will, He begins to reveal the ways He wants to use us. Sometimes, it might be clear from the start what our purpose is. Maybe you've always felt a passion for teaching, for helping others, or for sharing the gospel. But other times, discovering our purpose takes time, and it might evolve as we grow in our faith. The key is to trust God and to remain open to His guidance, knowing that He has a perfect plan for our lives that is far greater than anything we could imagine. Just as a birthmark grows with the person, our calling may grow and change over time, but the purpose behind it remains steady.

One of the most incredible things about God's purpose for our lives is that it is perfectly suited to who we are. He doesn't call us to do things that we're not equipped for. Instead, He equips us for the things He calls us to do. This is where faith comes in. Sometimes, we may feel inadequate or unprepared for what God is asking of us, but He has already given us the gifts we need, and He will continue to strengthen and guide us along the way. When we rely on our own strength, we may feel overwhelmed or unsure, but when we trust in God's power and grace, we can step into our calling with confidence, knowing that He will provide everything we need. Just as no one questions the existence or purpose of a birthmark, we shouldn't question the purpose that God has placed within us. It is there for a reason, and when we walk in that purpose, we bring glory to God and fulfillment to our own lives.

Another beautiful aspect of our purpose in Christ is that it is not just about us. God has designed our gifts and callings not only for our benefit but for the benefit of others. Each of us is part of a larger community, the body of Christ, and when we use our gifts, we build each other up and strengthen the church as a whole. Imagine how a birthmark, though small, is still part of the body it's on, contributing to that person's identity. In the same way, our unique gifts contribute to the identity of the church. Whether it's through teaching, serving, encouraging, giving, or simply showing kindness, we are called to use our gifts to bless those around us. And in doing so, we reflect the love of Christ to the world.

It's also important to remember that our purpose is not static. Just as birthmarks can change or evolve over time, so too can the ways in which God uses us. The purpose we have in one season of life may look different in another. For example, someone might be called to lead a Bible study for many years, and later, they may find that God is calling them to mentor younger believers or to focus on their family. The important thing is to remain open to how God is leading us and to trust that He knows the best ways to use our gifts in each stage of life. When we remain flexible and willing to follow God's direction, we find that He continues to use us in ways that bring us joy and fulfillment.

Sometimes, we may struggle with finding our purpose, especially during times when it feels like our gifts are being overlooked or underutilized. It can be easy to feel discouraged when we don't see immediate results or when it seems like others are being used in bigger, more visible ways. But we must remember that God's timing is perfect, and His plans for us are always good. Even in the seasons when we feel hidden or unnoticed, God is still working. He is still shaping us, preparing us, and using us in ways that we might not even realize. Just as a birthmark is always there, even when it's not immediately visible, our purpose in God remains, even when we don't see it clearly. Trusting in God's faithfulness and being patient in the waiting allows us to grow in ways that will make us even more effective when the time comes for our gifts to be fully used.

Another important aspect of purpose is that it is not about comparison. In today's world, it's easy to fall into the trap of comparing ourselves to others. We might look at someone who seems to be doing more for God and wonder why our own gifts aren't as big or as important. But just as no two birthmarks are the same, no two Christians are called to the same purpose. God has a unique plan for each of us, and we should never diminish the value of our own calling just because it looks different from someone else's. What matters is not how our gifts compare to others but how we are using the gifts God has given us. When we focus on being faithful with what we have, rather than comparing ourselves to others, we find true joy and fulfillment in walking in our purpose.

In the end, our purpose as believers is all about bringing glory to God. Whether we are called to preach to thousands, to encourage a friend, or to serve behind the scenes, our ultimate goal is to reflect the love and grace of Jesus to those around us. Our gifts are not given for our own benefit but to point others to Christ. When we use our gifts to serve others, we are living out the purpose God has for us, and we are fulfilling the role He created us to play in His Kingdom. Every action we take, every word we speak, and every choice we make can have an eternal impact when we are walking in our purpose.

In conclusion, just as birthmarks serve different purposes on the body, the gifts and callings that God gives each believer are unique and vital to His Kingdom. Romans 12:6 reminds us that we have "gifts differing according to the grace that is given to us," and this diversity of gifts is a beautiful reflection of God's creativity and His plan for His people. No matter how big or small our role may seem, it is important and valuable in the eyes of God. We are each created for a unique purpose, and when we walk in that purpose, we bring glory to God and fulfillment to our lives. Just as no two birthmarks are alike, no two Christians are called to the same journey, but together, we form the body of Christ, each playing our part in His great plan. Let us embrace the gifts we've been given, trust in God's plan for our lives, and walk confidently in the purpose He has for us, knowing that we are His workmanship, created in Christ Jesus for good works that He has prepared for us.

Chapter 6 – Process

The process of our spiritual journey is a lot like the texture of a birthmark. Just as some birthmarks are smooth, barely noticeable to the touch, while others are rough, raised, or bumpy, our walk with God takes us through different textures and experiences. Some seasons of our faith journey feel smooth and easy, when everything seems to be going well, and our trust in God flows naturally. We feel close to Him, and our path seems clear. But there are also rough seasons—times when life is hard, confusing, or painful, when nothing seems to go right, and it feels like we're walking on uneven ground. These rough seasons challenge us, testing our faith and making us question where God is in the midst of it all. Yet, both the smooth and the rough times are necessary. They are part of the process God uses to shape us, to refine us, and to grow us into the people He has called us to be. The rough textures in life don't mean that God has abandoned us; instead, they are often the times when He is working the most, refining our faith and deepening our trust in Him.

Just as no two birthmarks are exactly the same, no two spiritual journeys look alike. Each person's process is unique, and God leads each of us on a path that is perfectly suited to who we are and what He has planned for our lives. For some, the path may seem mostly smooth with only occasional bumps along the way. For others, the path may be filled with many more rough spots, but both kinds of journeys have a purpose. It's easy to want the smooth path, to wish that everything in life could be easy and without struggle. But the truth is, the rough spots are often where the deepest growth happens. Just like the rough texture of a birthmark is part of what makes it unique, the challenges and struggles we face are part of what makes our faith stronger and more resilient. The Bible tells us in 1 Peter 5:10, "But the God of all grace, who hath called us unto his eternal glory by Christ Jesus, after that ye have suffered a while, make you perfect, stablish, strengthen, settle you." This verse reminds us that God uses the hard times to perfect us, to strengthen us, and to make us more settled in our faith. The process might be difficult, but the end result is a deeper, stronger relationship with God.

Sometimes, when we are in the middle of a rough season, it can be hard to see the purpose in it. We may wonder why God is allowing us to go through such hard times, why our prayers don't seem to be answered, or why the path is so difficult. In those moments, it's easy to feel discouraged or even to doubt God's goodness. But just as a birthmark is a permanent part of someone's body, the struggles and challenges we face in life are a permanent part of our spiritual journey. They are not meant to break us but to build us up. When we trust God through the process, we can be confident that He is using even the hard times for our good. It's during the rough seasons that we learn to rely on God more deeply. When everything is going smoothly, it's easy to rely on our own strength, but when the road gets tough, we are reminded of how much we need God. We learn to lean on Him, to trust His plan even when we don't understand it, and to hold on to the hope that He is working things out for our good.

The process of our spiritual journey also involves waiting. Just as the texture of a birthmark doesn't change overnight, the work that God is doing in us takes time. We live in a world that wants quick results and instant answers, but God's timing is often different from our own. He is patient, and He calls us to be patient, too. In the smooth times, it's easy to feel like we're making progress and growing in our faith. But in the rough times, it can feel like we're stuck, like we're not moving forward at all. However, it's in these seasons of waiting, when we can't see what God is doing, that He is often doing His most important work. Just as a birthmark is formed over time, our spiritual growth happens gradually, as we go through the process of trusting God in every season.

One of the hardest parts of the process is dealing with pain. The rough texture of our lives often comes from the pain of loss, disappointment, failure, or betrayal. We may wonder why God allows us to experience such deep hurt, especially when we are trying to follow Him and live according to His will. But the pain we go through is not without purpose. It is in our pain that God meets us most intimately. He doesn't waste our pain; instead, He uses it to shape us into people who are more compassionate, more humble, and more reliant on His grace. Just as the rough spots on a birthmark are a part of its texture, the pain in our lives is a part of our story, and God uses it to write a beautiful narrative of redemption and hope.

Another important aspect of the process is that it's not something we go through alone. Just as a birthmark is part of the body, our spiritual journey is part of the body of Christ. We are not meant to walk this path by ourselves. God places people in our lives to encourage us, to pray for us, and to help us along the way. Sometimes, when the road gets rough, it can be easy to isolate ourselves, to feel like no one else understands what we're going through. But God has given us the gift of community, of brothers and sisters in Christ who can walk with us through both the smooth and the rough seasons. They can remind us of God's faithfulness when we're struggling to see it for ourselves, and they can offer support and encouragement when we feel like giving up. The process of our spiritual journey is something that we walk together, as the body of Christ.

The process also involves surrender. Just as we cannot control the texture of a birthmark, we cannot control every aspect of our spiritual journey. There will be times when God calls us to surrender our plans, our desires, and our sense of control to Him. This can be one of the hardest parts of the process because we often want things to go a certain way, and when they don't, we can feel frustrated or disappointed. But God asks us to trust Him, to believe that His ways are higher than our ways and that His plan is better than anything we could come up with on our own. When we surrender to God's process, we open ourselves up to the incredible work He wants to do in our lives. It may not always look the way we expected, but it will always be for our good and for His glory.

The process of our spiritual journey also involves transformation. Just as the texture of a birthmark is part of what makes it unique, the ups and downs of our journey are part of what makes us who we are in Christ. Over time, as we go through both the smooth and the rough seasons, we are transformed into people who look more like Jesus. This transformation is not always easy. It often requires us to let go of old habits, to confront sin in our lives, and to allow God to shape us in ways that may be uncomfortable. But the end result is something beautiful. We become people who reflect the love, grace, and truth of Christ to the world around us. The process may be long, and it may be difficult, but it is worth it because it leads to a deeper relationship with God and a life that glorifies Him.

In conclusion, the texture of a birthmark is a powerful metaphor for the process of our spiritual journey. Some parts of the journey are smooth and easy, while others are rough and difficult. But both are necessary for our growth and for the refining of our faith. As 1 Peter 5:10 reminds us, God uses the rough times to make us perfect, to strengthen us, and to settle us in our faith. The process is not always easy, but it is always purposeful. Whether we are in a season of smooth sailing or walking through a rough patch, we can trust that God is at work in our lives, shaping us into the people He has called us to be. He is with us every step of the way, and He promises that the process will lead to something beautiful. So let us embrace the process, knowing that God is using every part of our journey to refine us, to strengthen us, and to draw us closer to Him. The road may be rough at times, but the destination is worth it. God is faithful, and He will complete the good work He has begun in us.

Chapter 7 – Progression

Our faith journey, much like a birthmark, goes through changes over time, reflecting the natural process of growth, learning, and transformation. Just as a birthmark may change in appearance as a person grows, darkening or becoming more defined, our relationship with God progresses as we mature in our understanding of His love, grace, and purpose for our lives. When we first come to know Christ, our faith might feel new and exciting, but also a bit like uncharted territory. We are filled with wonder and passion, but there is so much we don't yet understand. Over time, however, our faith begins to deepen as we face life's challenges, learn from God's Word, and experience His presence in both the joyful and difficult moments. The progression of faith is not always a straight line; there are highs and lows, times of great clarity and times of confusion, moments of strength and moments of weakness. But through it all, God is guiding us, helping us to grow, just as a gardener carefully tends to a plant, nurturing it from a seed into full bloom. This process is ongoing, and it never truly ends because there is always more to learn about God's endless grace and love.

In 2 Peter 3:18, we are reminded to "grow in grace, and in the knowledge of our Lord and Saviour Jesus Christ." This verse highlights the fact that growth in our spiritual lives is not something that happens passively. We are called to be active participants in this progression, seeking to know God more deeply and allowing His grace to shape us. Just as a birthmark might change gradually over the years, our faith matures through the small, everyday experiences that God uses to mold us into the people He has called us to be. Each day brings new opportunities to trust Him more, to rely on His strength, and to let go of the things that hold us back. This growth doesn't always come easily—just as a child's growth can sometimes be accompanied by growing pains, our spiritual progression can involve discomfort as we face trials, confront our own shortcomings, or step out in faith when we are uncertain. But these moments of challenge are essential to our growth because they push us beyond our comfort zones and force us to depend on God in ways we wouldn't otherwise.

At the beginning of our Christian walk, much like a baby first learning to walk, we may stumble and fall frequently. We might be unsure of how to live out our faith in the real world, uncertain of what it looks like to truly follow Jesus day by day. But as we spend more time with God—through prayer, reading Scripture, and learning from others—we begin to gain our footing. We start to understand what it means to trust God in all things, to live in a way that reflects His love, and to seek His will above our own. This progression is a process of learning, one step at a time. Sometimes the lessons come through joyous moments, like when we experience an answer to prayer or see God's hand at work in our lives. Other times, the lessons come through hardship, when we face trials that test our faith and force us to cling to God even when we don't understand why things are happening the way they are. It is in these moments of trial that our faith is refined and strengthened. Just as fire refines gold, burning away impurities, the challenges we face in life can refine our faith, removing the things that hinder us from fully trusting in God.

Progression in faith also means letting go of old ways of thinking and living. When we first become Christians, we bring with us habits, attitudes, and beliefs that don't align with the new life we've been given in Christ. Over time, as we grow, God gently works in our hearts, helping us to shed those old ways and embrace the new identity He has given us. This process of transformation is gradual, much like how a birthmark might slowly change shape or color over the years. It doesn't happen all at once, and sometimes it can be frustrating when we don't see immediate results. But we can trust that God is faithfully working in us, even when we can't see the changes right away. Philippians 1:6 tells us that "He who began a good work in you will carry it on to completion until the day of Christ Jesus." This promise reminds us that God is not finished with us yet. He is constantly working to make us more like Jesus, and He will not stop until that work is complete.

As we grow in our faith, we also begin to see the world differently. Our perspective shifts as we come to understand more of God's heart and His purposes for the world. Things that once seemed important—material success, the approval of others, worldly accomplishments—begin to lose their hold on us as we realize that true fulfillment comes from knowing and serving God. We start to value the things that God values: love, kindness, humility, and justice. Our hearts become more aligned with His, and we begin to see people through His eyes, recognizing their worth and loving them as He loves us. This change in perspective is a key part of our spiritual progression because it moves us away from a self-centered way of living and towards a life that is focused on glorifying God and serving others.

One of the beautiful things about the progression of faith is that it allows us to look back and see how far we've come. Just as we can look at old photos and notice how much a birthmark has changed over the years, we can reflect on our spiritual journey and see the ways God has grown us. We can see the ways He has answered prayers, the lessons He has taught us, and the ways He has provided for us in difficult times. This reflection fills us with gratitude and reminds us of God's faithfulness. Even when the road has been tough, God has been with us every step of the way, guiding us and helping us to grow. This awareness of God's past faithfulness gives us confidence as we continue to move forward, knowing that He will continue to be with us as we progress in our faith.

As we grow, we also begin to understand more deeply the grace of God. At first, we might only have a surface-level understanding of grace, seeing it as God's forgiveness of our sins. But as we progress, we come to realize that grace is so much more than that. Grace is God's unmerited favor, His kindness towards us, not because of anything we've done but simply because of His love for us. It's the grace that sustains us through difficult times, the grace that gives us strength when we are weak, the grace that enables us to forgive others, and the grace that keeps us going when we feel like giving up. Growing in grace, as Peter urges us to do, means learning to rely more and more on God's strength and less on our own. It means accepting that we are imperfect and that we will make mistakes, but that God's grace is always there to pick us up and help us move forward.

Another important part of the progression of faith is learning to trust God more deeply. At the beginning of our journey, we might trust God with some things but hold back in other areas. We might say we trust Him, but when challenges come, we find ourselves relying on our own understanding or trying to control the situation ourselves. As we grow in faith, however, we learn to let go of that need for control and to trust God fully, even when things don't make sense. This kind of trust comes with experience. The more we see God's faithfulness in our lives, the easier it becomes to trust Him in the future. Over time, we develop a deep sense of peace, knowing that no matter what happens, God is in control and He is working all things together for our good.

Finally, the progression of faith is not just about personal growth; it's about being transformed so that we can help others on their journey. As we mature in our relationship with God, we are called to encourage and support others who are walking the same path. Just as someone who has gone through a difficult season can offer comfort and wisdom to someone going through the same thing, we are called to use the lessons we've learned to help others grow in their faith. This is one of the ways that God works through us to build up the body of Christ. Our progression is not just for our benefit but for the benefit of others. As we grow, we become more equipped to serve, to lead, and to be a light in the world.

In conclusion, just as birthmarks change over time, a Christian's faith progresses and matures through the process of growth, learning, and experience. This progression is not always easy, and it often involves challenges, setbacks, and growing pains. But it is a beautiful process that brings us closer to God and helps us become more like Jesus. As we grow in grace and in the knowledge of our Lord and Savior, we learn to trust Him more deeply, to see the world through His eyes, and to rely on His strength instead of our own. We are transformed, not just for our own sake but so that we can encourage and support others in their faith journey. The progression of faith is a lifelong process, but we can trust that God is with us every step of the way, guiding us, shaping us, and helping us to grow into the people He has created us to be.

Chapter 8 – Pedigree

Just as birthmarks can be passed down through family lines, our spiritual lives can be influenced by the faith of those who came before us. Many of us are blessed to come from families with a strong spiritual pedigree, where parents, grandparents, or other relatives have walked with God, prayed for us, and taught us about Jesus from a young age. Having a family heritage of faith is a precious gift. It gives us a foundation of knowledge, values, and support that can guide us through life. For many, this heritage is like an inheritance, a birthright of sorts, passed down from one generation to the next. We may have been raised in church, heard Bible stories from the time we were little, and learned to pray at our parents' knees. However, just as a birthmark might be inherited, yet is uniquely ours, our relationship with God cannot simply be inherited or passed down. Each person must come to know Jesus personally. No matter how faithful our parents or grandparents may have been, their faith cannot substitute for our own. Every believer must choose to follow Christ for themselves, and every person's walk with God will be unique.

John 1:12 says, "But as many as received him, to them gave he power to become the sons of God, even to them that believe on his name." This verse reminds us that becoming a child of God is not something that happens automatically, even if we come from a family of believers. It's a personal decision that each of us must make. God doesn't have grandchildren; He only has sons and daughters. This means that while our spiritual heritage can be a blessing and a guide, it cannot be a substitute for a real, personal relationship with Jesus. At some point, each of us must decide for ourselves to receive Him, to believe in His name, and to commit our lives to following Him.

Having a family legacy of faith is a great starting point, but it's not the whole story. Some people might grow up in homes where faith is the central part of life, and they can trace their Christian heritage back for generations. Others might come from families where faith was never talked about, or where belief in God was even discouraged. Still, others might have a mix, with one parent or grandparent who was a believer and others who were not. No matter where we come from, each of us is given the opportunity to develop our own personal relationship with God. This journey is different for everyone. For those who come from a long line of believers, there can be a certain sense of comfort in knowing that others in their family have walked the same path. But for those who don't have that background, there can also be a beautiful sense of discovery in being the first in their family to find faith, to break new ground, and to start a new spiritual legacy for the generations that follow.

The truth is, no matter what kind of spiritual pedigree we have, every Christian must walk their own journey with God. It's wonderful to have the prayers and guidance of family members who have gone before us, but those things are only meant to point us in the right direction. Ultimately, we must build our own relationship with God through prayer, reading His Word, and experiencing His presence for ourselves. It's like having a roadmap but still needing to take the journey ourselves. No one can take those steps of faith for us. And while our family's faith might help us get started, it's up to us to decide how we will live out our own faith in the day-to-day realities of life.

Sometimes, having a strong spiritual heritage can even bring challenges. There can be expectations to live up to, or pressure to follow in the footsteps of those who came before us. For example, if your parents were deeply involved in ministry, you might feel pressure to do the same, even if God is calling you in a different direction. Or, if you come from a family that was very strict in its faith, you might wrestle with finding your own way to express your beliefs. But God doesn't call us to replicate someone else's faith. He calls us to be uniquely who He created us to be. Just like a birthmark may be inherited but has its own unique shape and appearance, our faith may be influenced by our family, but it must take on a form that is true to who we are and what God has called us to do.

On the other hand, for those who don't come from a family of faith, it can sometimes feel like they are starting from scratch. They might not have the same foundation that others have, and that can feel daunting. But the beauty of the gospel is that it is available to everyone, no matter their background. Whether you come from a long line of believers or you are the first person in your family to follow Christ, the promise is the same: When you receive Him and believe in

His name, you become a child of God. Your past, your family history, and your background don't determine your future with God. He welcomes everyone into His family, and once you are His, you are part of a new spiritual lineage that stretches back to the very beginning of time.

For those who are the first in their family to follow Christ, there is a special kind of joy in knowing that you are paving the way for future generations. Your decision to follow Jesus can change the course of your family's history. The prayers you pray, the faith you live out, and the love you show can influence your children, your grandchildren, and beyond. Even if you didn't inherit a spiritual legacy, you can create one. And for those who come from a family of believers, you have the opportunity to continue the legacy of faith that was passed down to you, to build on the foundation that was laid by those who came before you, and to pass it on to the next generation in an even stronger way.

One of the amazing things about God is that He uses both our heritage and our personal experiences to shape us into who He wants us to be. For some, their family's faith will serve as a rock-solid foundation that they build on throughout their lives. For others, their journey may be more about discovering faith for themselves, without the help of a spiritual pedigree. But in both cases, God is faithful. He is able to take the seeds that were planted by others in our lives and help them grow, or He can plant new seeds in hearts that have never known Him before. The process is different for everyone, but the result is the same: a relationship with the living God that is personal, real, and life-changing.

It's important to remember that while family can provide guidance and support, our relationship with God is deeply personal. There are times when we will need to seek God on our own, to wrestle with questions and doubts, and to find answers in His Word. We can't rely on our family's faith to carry us through difficult times. When life gets hard, when we face challenges or disappointments, it's our own relationship with God that will sustain us. It's in those moments that we learn to lean on Him, to trust Him, and to experience His presence for ourselves.

John 1:12 emphasizes that becoming a child of God is a personal choice: "But as many as received him, to them gave he power to become the sons of God, even to them that believe on his name." This verse reminds us that receiving Jesus is an individual act of faith. It's not something that can be done for us by our parents, grandparents, or anyone else. We must each come to a point where we decide to accept Jesus into our lives and commit to following Him. It's a decision that changes everything, but it's also a decision that must be made by each person on their own.

At the same time, our spiritual heritage can be a great source of encouragement. Knowing that we come from a family of believers can give us a sense of belonging and strength. It's comforting to know that others have walked the path of faith before us and that we are part of a larger story. Their example can inspire us to keep going when we feel discouraged, and their prayers can support us in ways we may not even realize. But even with this support, we must still cultivate our own relationship with God. It's through spending time with Him, reading His Word, and praying that we grow in our faith and become who He has called us to be.

In conclusion, just as birthmarks may be inherited, our spiritual heritage may come from a family of faith, but every believer must develop their own relationship with God. Whether we come from a long line of believers or we are the first in our family to follow Christ, the decision to receive Him is a personal one. Our family's faith can provide a strong foundation, but it is up to us to build on that foundation and to walk our own journey with God. As John 1:12 reminds us, when we receive Jesus, we are given the power to become children of God—sons and daughters who are loved, valued, and called to live out their faith in a way that is uniquely ours. Whether our spiritual pedigree is long or short, God has a plan for each of us, and it is through our personal relationship with Him that we discover who we are and what He has created us to do. So let us embrace the spiritual heritage we have been given, while also seeking to know God for ourselves, growing in our faith, and walking the path He has set before us.

Chapter 9 – Passing

Just as some birthmarks naturally fade over time, the struggles, sins, and brokenness of our old life begin to fade away when we are renewed in Christ. When we first come to know Jesus, it's like stepping into the light for the very first time, and all the things that used to define us—the mistakes we made, the hurts we carried, the sins that weighed us down—start to lose their grip on our hearts. These things, once so familiar and deeply ingrained in who we were, begin to fade as we grow closer to Him. It doesn't always happen all at once. Much like a birthmark that slowly fades, the process of letting go of our old nature is often gradual. It takes time, and it can be a difficult journey. We might not see the changes day by day, but little by little, God works in us, transforming our hearts and minds, renewing our spirit, and shaping us into the people He created us to be. The old ways of thinking, the old habits, the shame, and the guilt begin to pass away, and in their place, new life, hope, and peace start to take root. This process is one of the most beautiful aspects of our walk with God, because it's a testament to His grace and His power to change us from the inside out.

2 Corinthians 5:17 tells us, "Therefore if any man be in Christ, he is a new creature: old things are passed away; behold, all things are become new." This verse is a powerful reminder that when we are in Christ, we are not just improved versions of ourselves; we are entirely new creations. Our past no longer defines us. The things that once held us back, the sins that once enslaved us, and the struggles that once seemed insurmountable no longer have the same hold on us. Instead, they begin to fade into the background as we focus more and more on who we are in Christ. This passing away of our old nature is not just about leaving behind bad behaviors; it's about a total transformation of our heart, mind, and soul. We begin to see ourselves differently, not as people defined by our mistakes or failures, but as children of God, loved, forgiven, and set free. The more we

understand this truth, the more our old ways lose their power over us, and the more we are able to walk in the newness of life that Christ offers.

But just like a birthmark that fades gradually, this transformation is often a process. When we first come to Christ, we bring with us all the baggage from our old life. We may still struggle with temptations, habits, or thought patterns that are hard to break. We might still wrestle with feelings of guilt, shame, or unworthiness because of the things we've done in the past. But as we grow in our relationship with God, He gently works on us, helping us to let go of these things, one by one. The more we spend time in His Word, the more we learn to trust Him, the more we allow His Spirit to work in us, the more these old things pass away. It's not always easy, and there will be times when we feel like we're taking two steps forward and one step back. But God is faithful, and He promises to complete the good work He has begun in us. He doesn't expect us to change overnight, and He doesn't abandon us when we fall short. Instead, He walks with us every step of the way, helping us to shed our old nature and embrace the new life He has given us.

One of the most amazing things about this process is that it's not just about external changes. Yes, our actions and behaviors begin to reflect our new life in Christ, but the deeper transformation happens in our hearts. We start to desire different things. The things that used to tempt us, the things that once seemed so important, begin to lose their appeal. Our hearts are changed, and with that change comes new desires, new priorities, and a new perspective on life. We begin to see the world through the eyes of Christ, with more love, more compassion, more patience, and more grace. The things that once caused us to stumble start to fade, not because we are trying harder, but because God is changing us from the inside out. It's a transformation that we could never achieve on our own, but with God's help, it becomes possible.

As we grow closer to God, the struggles of our old life continue to lose their grip on us. This doesn't mean that we'll never face temptation or that we'll be perfect. We will still face challenges, and we will still stumble from time to time. But the difference is that we are no longer slaves to our old nature. We are no longer defined by our past mistakes or trapped by our old sins. We have been set free, and with that freedom comes the ability to choose a new way of living. The more we walk with God, the more we experience His grace, and the more we understand the depth of His love for us, the easier it becomes to let go of the things that used to hold us back. The things we once struggled with no longer have the same power over us because we have something far greater—Jesus Christ.

This passing away of our old nature also brings a deep sense of peace. There is peace in knowing that our past does not define us. There is peace in knowing that we don't have to carry the weight of our mistakes any longer. There is peace in knowing that we are forgiven, loved, and accepted by God, not because of what we've done, but because of what Christ has done for us. This peace allows us to move forward with confidence, knowing that God is with us, that He is for us, and that He is transforming us day by day. It allows us to live without fear of the past or anxiety about the future because we know that our identity is secure in Christ.

The fading of our old life and the passing away of our old nature also brings hope. It reminds us that no matter how far we've fallen, no matter how many mistakes we've made, there is always hope for redemption. In Christ, there is always the promise of new beginnings, of second chances, of grace that is greater than our sins. This hope gives us the strength to keep going, even when the road is hard, even when the changes are slow, even when we feel like we're not making progress. We can have hope because we know that God is not finished with us yet. He is still at work, and He will not stop until we are fully transformed into the image of His Son.

This transformation is not just for us, but it also affects those around us. As our old nature fades away and we become more like Christ, the people in our lives begin to see the difference. Our families, our friends, our coworkers—they see the changes in us. They see the peace we have, the joy we carry, the love we show. And through these changes, they are drawn to the One who is making those changes possible. Our lives become a testimony to the power of God's grace and His ability to transform even the most broken, messed-up people into new creations. This is one of the most beautiful parts of our transformation: that God uses it not only to change us but to reach others as well.

In conclusion, just as some birthmarks fade over time, so too do the struggles and sins of our old life when we are renewed in Christ. As 2 Corinthians 5:17 says, "Therefore if any man be in Christ, he is a new creature: old things are passed away; behold, all things are become new." This is the promise of the gospel: that no matter who we were, no matter what we've done, we are made new in Christ. Our old nature, with all its struggles and sins, begins to pass away as we grow closer to Him. This process is not always easy, and it doesn't happen overnight, but God is faithful to complete the work He has started in us. He is with us every step of the way, helping us to let go of our old life and embrace the new life He has given us. And as we walk with Him, we experience the peace, joy, and hope that come from knowing that we are loved, forgiven, and set free. So let us continue to grow in our relationship with Christ, knowing that the old has passed away and that all things have become new.

Chapter 10 – Problem

Just as some birthmarks can cause medical problems if they are left untreated, certain spiritual issues in our lives can create serious problems in our walk with Christ if we ignore them or try to hide them. At first, a small issue—whether it's a sin we keep secret, an unresolved hurt, a wrong attitude, or a habit we know doesn't honor God—might seem harmless or insignificant. We might think, "It's not a big deal," or, "I'll deal with it later." But just as an untreated medical problem can grow worse over time, spiritual issues that go unaddressed can slowly damage our relationship with God and with others. They can weaken our faith, steal our joy, and hold us back from experiencing the fullness of life that God has for us. Much like how a birthmark might need medical attention to prevent complications, spiritual issues need to be addressed with prayer, confession, and wise counsel before they cause deeper harm. The Bible reminds us of the importance of this in James 5:16, which says, "Confess your faults one to another, and pray one for another, that ye may be healed. The effectual fervent prayer of a righteous man availeth much." This verse shows us that healing—whether physical or spiritual—often begins with confession and prayer. When we bring our problems into the light, admit our faults, and seek God's help, healing can begin.

One of the reasons we avoid dealing with spiritual problems is because it can be uncomfortable to face them. Just as going to the doctor might make us anxious, confronting the spiritual issues in our lives can make us feel vulnerable or even ashamed. We might fear what others will think if they knew what we were struggling with, or we might be afraid of admitting that we don't have it all together. But hiding our struggles only makes things worse. The longer we try to ignore the problems, the more they grow. Sin has a way of spreading like an untreated infection, touching every part of our lives if we let it. It affects our relationship with God, making us feel distant from Him, and it affects our relationships with others, causing division, mistrust, and pain. But when we choose to be honest about our struggles and bring them into the light, we give God the chance to heal and restore us. There is great power in confession, not only to God but to trusted people who can walk with us and pray for us. That's why James 5:16 encourages us to confess our faults to one another. It's not about shaming ourselves or airing our dirty laundry for the world to see—it's about creating a space where healing can begin.

One of the biggest spiritual problems that often goes unchecked is unconfessed sin. Whether it's a sin that we're actively committing or one from the past that we've never dealt with, unconfessed sin creates a barrier between us and God. It might not seem like a big deal at first, but over time, that unconfessed sin weighs on our hearts. It creates feelings of guilt and shame that can pull us away from God. The more we try to hide it or ignore it, the harder it becomes to pray, to worship, and to feel close to God. Our spiritual life starts to feel dry, and we might wonder why we don't feel the same connection with God that we once had. The truth is, God is always ready and willing to forgive us, but we need to be willing to bring our sins to Him. When we confess our sins, He is faithful and just to forgive us and cleanse us from all unrighteousness, as 1 John 1:9 tells us. There is freedom in confession. It lifts the weight off our shoulders and allows us to experience God's grace in a powerful way. But confession is only the first step—repentance must follow. Just as a birthmark that causes a medical issue might need treatment or surgery, spiritual problems need to be addressed with intentional actions, not just words. We need to turn away from the sin and seek God's help to overcome it.

Another spiritual problem that can go unchecked is unresolved hurt or bitterness. When someone hurts us, it's natural to feel angry or upset, but if we hold on to those feelings and let them fester, they can turn into bitterness that poisons our hearts. Bitterness is like a spiritual toxin that affects every part of our lives. It makes us bitter not only toward the person who hurt us but toward others as well. It can make it hard to trust people, to love freely, and to experience the joy that God wants us to have. Bitterness also creates distance between us and God because it hardens our hearts. When we hold on to bitterness, we're holding on to unforgiveness, and unforgiveness blocks the flow of God's grace in our lives. Jesus calls us to forgive others, just as He has forgiven us. Forgiveness doesn't mean excusing the wrong or pretending it didn't hurt—it means choosing to release the person from the debt they owe us and trusting God to heal the pain. When we forgive, we open the door to healing, both in our relationships and in our own hearts.

Sometimes, the spiritual problems we face aren't the result of sin or hurt but come from wrong attitudes or beliefs. Maybe we've allowed pride to creep in, making us think we can handle everything on our own. Maybe we've started to believe the lie that we're not good enough, that God could never really love us or use us. These wrong attitudes and beliefs might seem harmless at first, but they can deeply affect our walk with God if they go unchecked. Pride can keep us from relying on God, causing us to make decisions without seeking His guidance, and can lead to spiritual burnout. Believing lies about ourselves can make us doubt God's love and grace, leading to feelings of unworthiness and hopelessness. These attitudes need to be confronted with the truth of God's Word. When we immerse ourselves in Scripture, we are reminded of who God is and who we are in Him. The Bible tells us that we are loved, chosen, and forgiven. We are reminded that we are not alone, and that God is our strength and our guide. When we replace lies with truth, our spiritual health is restored.

Another common spiritual problem is the tendency to isolate ourselves when we're struggling. It's easy to pull away from others when we're going through a hard time, especially when we feel ashamed or overwhelmed by our struggles. We might think that no one else would understand, or we might fear judgment or rejection if we open up. But isolation is one of the enemy's most effective tactics. When we're alone, we become more vulnerable to temptation, discouragement, and despair. The Bible tells us that we need one another—that we are part of the body of Christ, and just as a body can't function properly when one part is disconnected, we can't thrive spiritually when we're disconnected from the community of believers. We need the support, encouragement, and accountability that come from being in fellowship with other Christians. That's why James 5:16 emphasizes the importance of praying for one another. When we share our struggles with trusted friends and ask for their prayers, we invite God's healing power into our lives. Prayer is a powerful weapon in the fight against spiritual problems. It connects us with God, aligns our hearts with His, and invites His Spirit to work in us. The prayers of others strengthen us and remind us that we're not alone in the battle.

Spiritual problems don't just go away on their own. Just like a medical issue won't heal without treatment, spiritual issues need to be addressed with intentionality. This is where wise counsel comes in. Sometimes, we need the wisdom and guidance of mature Christians, pastors, or counselors to help us navigate through our struggles. These people can offer us biblical wisdom, pray with us, and help us find practical ways to overcome the issues we're facing. They can provide perspective, helping us see things we might have missed, and they can offer encouragement when we feel discouraged. Seeking counsel isn't a sign of weakness—it's a recognition that we all need help from time to time. God often uses other people to bring about healing and restoration in our lives. When we seek out counsel and allow others to speak into our lives, we're opening ourselves up to the work that God wants to do in us.

In conclusion, just as some birthmarks can cause medical problems, certain spiritual issues, if left unchecked, can create serious problems in our walk with Christ. Whether it's unconfessed sin, unresolved hurt, wrong attitudes, or isolation, these issues can prevent us from experiencing the fullness of life that God has for us. But when we address these problems with prayer, confession, and wise counsel, healing and restoration can begin. James 5:16 reminds us of the importance of confessing our faults to one another and praying for one another so that we may be healed. God doesn't want us to carry the weight of our struggles alone—He offers us His grace, His healing, and His strength to overcome. As we bring our spiritual problems into the light, we allow God to work in us, transforming us and drawing us closer to Him. The process might be uncomfortable, but the result is freedom, healing, and a deeper relationship with God. So let us not ignore the spiritual issues in our lives, but instead, let us bring them to God in prayer, seek the counsel of others, and trust that God is faithful to heal, restore, and renew us.

Chapter 11 – Prescription

Just as there are treatments for birthmarks that cause discomfort or problems, God offers a prescription for the spiritual discomforts and sins that burden our hearts. Life can often feel like we are walking around with hidden pain, whether it's emotional wounds, sins we haven't dealt with, or just a sense of distance from God. Sometimes, just like a birthmark can cause irritation or embarrassment, spiritual discomfort can weigh heavily on us, making it hard to experience the peace, joy, and fullness of life that God intends for us. But the good news is that God provides the remedy for every one of these struggles. He doesn't leave us to carry our burdens alone. He offers healing, forgiveness, and freedom, and the prescription for that healing is found in His Word and through His Spirit. Psalm 107:20 says, "He sent his word, and healed them, and delivered them from their destructions." This verse reminds us that God's Word has the power to heal us from whatever is hurting or holding us back, and it's His Spirit that works within us to transform our hearts and lead us into a place of restoration and wholeness.

Sometimes, we carry spiritual discomfort for so long that we start to believe that it's just something we have to live with, like a birthmark that causes irritation but seems permanent. We might think, "This is just the way I am," or, "I'll never be free from this," whether we're talking about a recurring sin, an emotional wound from the past, or a deep sense of shame or guilt. But God doesn't want us to live with spiritual pain. He wants to heal us, to set us free from the things that weigh us down, and to give us a new life filled with His peace. Just as a doctor might prescribe medicine or treatment to heal a physical issue, God prescribes His Word and the work of His Spirit as the ultimate remedy for our souls. His Word is like spiritual medicine that goes deep into our hearts, bringing healing to the broken places and delivering us from the destructive patterns that have taken hold of our lives. The Bible is full of truth that can set us free, if we are willing to receive it.

One of the most common sources of spiritual discomfort is sin. Whether it's a sin we keep falling into or a sin from our past that we can't seem to move on from, sin creates a barrier between us and God. It leaves us feeling ashamed, distant, and often trapped in a cycle of guilt. We may try to deal with it on our own, but the more we try to fix things ourselves, the more frustrated we become. This is where God's prescription comes in. He offers us forgiveness and freedom from sin, not through our own efforts but through the finished work of Jesus Christ on the cross. When we confess our sins to God and ask for His forgiveness, He is faithful and just to forgive us and cleanse us from all unrighteousness (1 John 1:9). This forgiveness isn't something we have to earn; it's a free gift, and it brings immediate relief from the burden of guilt that sin creates. God's prescription for sin is simple: repentance and trust in His grace. When we turn away from our sin and turn toward God, we are met with open arms and the healing power of His love. No matter how deep our sin goes, God's grace goes deeper, and His Word assures us that we are forgiven and made new.

Another area where we often feel spiritual discomfort is in the wounds we carry from the past. Whether it's the result of someone else's actions or the consequences of our own choices, emotional and spiritual wounds can leave us feeling broken and stuck. We may try to cover them up or push them down, hoping that time will heal them, but without addressing them, they continue to fester beneath the surface. God's prescription for these wounds is found in His Word, which speaks healing to our souls. The Bible tells us that God is near to the brokenhearted and saves those who are crushed in spirit (Psalm 34:18). He knows the depth of our pain, and He cares deeply about our healing. His Word is filled with promises that remind us of His love, His faithfulness, and His ability to heal even the deepest wounds. But more than that, God invites us to bring our pain to Him in prayer. When we pour out our hearts to Him, when we are honest about our hurt and our need for healing, He meets us in those moments and begins the process of restoration. Just as a prescription for a physical illness might take time to work, spiritual healing is often a process, but God is patient, and He walks with us every step of the way.

God's Spirit is also a vital part of the prescription for spiritual discomfort. While His Word gives us the truth we need, His Spirit works within us to apply that truth to our lives. The Holy Spirit is our Comforter, our Guide, and the One who gives us strength when we are weak. When we feel lost, confused, or overwhelmed, the Holy Spirit is there to remind us of God's presence and to lead us back to the path of peace. One of the ways the Spirit works in our lives is by convicting us of sin and leading us to repentance. This conviction isn't about making us feel condemned or ashamed; it's about guiding us toward healing and freedom. The Spirit gently reveals the areas of our lives where we need to change and helps us to let go of the things that are causing spiritual discomfort. He empowers us to make those changes, giving us the strength we need to walk in obedience to God's Word. According to Philippians 4:7, The Holy Spirit also fills us with the peace of God, a peace that surpasses all understanding and guards our hearts and minds in Christ Jesus.

There are also times when our spiritual discomfort comes from a sense of emptiness or a lack of direction. We might feel like we're drifting, unsure of our purpose or distant from God's presence. In these moments, God's prescription is to draw near to Him through prayer and worship. When we seek God with all our hearts, He promises to meet us where we are. Prayer is a powerful tool that connects us with the heart of God and allows us to experience His presence in a tangible way. Worship, too, has the ability to shift our focus from our problems to the greatness of God. When we lift our eyes to Him in worship, we are reminded of His power, His goodness, and His love for us. The more we seek God, the more we will find Him, and the more our spiritual discomfort will be replaced by the joy and peace that come from being in His presence.

Sometimes, the spiritual discomfort we feel is because we are not living in alignment with God's will for our lives. We might be chasing after things that are outside of His plan for us, or we might be holding on to things that He's asking us to let go of. This kind of discomfort is often a sign that God is calling us to realign our lives with His purpose. His Word is the prescription that helps us see where we've gone off track and guides us back to where we need to be. The Bible is filled with wisdom and instruction for how to live a life that honors God and brings us true fulfillment. When we study His Word and listen to His Spirit, we are able to discern His will for our lives and make the necessary changes. This might involve letting go of certain habits, relationships, or ambitions that are not in line with God's plan, but the result is a life of greater peace and purpose.

In conclusion, just as there are treatments for birthmarks that cause discomfort, God provides a prescription for the spiritual discomforts we face in life. His Word is the ultimate remedy, filled with truth that heals, restores, and sets us free. Psalm 107:20 reminds us that God sent His Word to heal us and deliver us from our destructions. Whether we are struggling with sin, emotional wounds, confusion, or a sense of emptiness, God has provided everything we need for healing and wholeness through His Word and His Spirit. We don't have to live with spiritual discomfort; we don't have to carry the weight of our burdens alone. God invites us to come to Him, to confess our sins, to bring our pain, and to seek His wisdom and guidance. When we follow His prescription, we experience the healing that only He can provide. It may not always happen overnight, and the process may require patience and perseverance, but God is faithful, and He promises to walk with us every step of the way. The more we immerse ourselves in His Word and allow His Spirit to work in us, the more we will find the peace, joy, and freedom that come from living in alignment with His will. So let us turn to God with every area of spiritual discomfort, trusting that He is the Great Physician who knows exactly what we need for healing and wholeness. His Word is the prescription that brings life, and His Spirit is the power that transforms us from the inside out. Let us embrace the healing that God offers and walk in the newness of life that comes from being fully surrendered to Him.

Chapter 12 – Perception

Just as birthmarks can affect how we feel about ourselves and how others see us, living boldly for Christ can also have an impact on our self-esteem and how we are perceived by the world. Birthmarks, especially those that are more visible, can sometimes make people feel self-conscious, leading to feelings of insecurity or a fear of being judged by others. In the same way, when we choose to live openly as Christians and stand firm in our faith, it can sometimes make us feel exposed or vulnerable to the opinions of others. There may be moments when we feel out of place, judged, or even rejected because of our commitment to Christ. Living for Jesus in a world that often opposes or misunderstands our faith can be challenging, and at times, it might feel like we're walking against the tide. We might worry about how people will react when they see us living differently, making choices based on our beliefs, and standing up for what's right according to God's Word. But just as someone with a birthmark can learn to embrace their unique appearance, we can learn to embrace our identity in Christ with confidence. Our true worth is not found in how others see us, but in how God sees us. Galatians 3:26 tells us, "For ye are all the children of God by faith in Christ Jesus." This verse is a powerful reminder that our identity is rooted in the fact that we are children of God, and that is where our confidence comes from.

The world places so much emphasis on appearance, success, and fitting in, and it can be easy to feel like we don't measure up if we don't conform to those standards. Just like how a birthmark can make someone feel different or less than, our faith can sometimes make us feel like we don't fit in with the crowd. We might face pressure to blend in, to downplay our beliefs, or to go along with what everyone else is doing, just to avoid standing out. But when we know who we are in Christ, we can stand firm, even when it's hard. We are not defined by the world's standards or by what others think of us. We are defined by our relationship with Jesus. As children of God, we are loved, accepted, and valued beyond measure. Our confidence doesn't come from external things like popularity, appearance, or approval—it comes from knowing that we belong to God and that nothing can change that.

Living boldly for Christ means being willing to be different, even when it's uncomfortable. Just as someone with a birthmark might learn to accept and even appreciate what makes them unique, we can learn to appreciate the uniqueness of being set apart as followers of Jesus. We are called to be the light of the world, to shine in the darkness, and to live in a way that reflects God's love and truth. This calling means that we won't always fit in with the world's expectations, and that's okay. In fact, we are not meant to fit in. Romans 12:2 tells us, "Do not conform to the pattern of this world, but be transformed by the renewing of your mind." Our goal is not to blend in with the world, but to stand out for Christ, showing others what it means to live a life of love, grace, and truth. This can sometimes lead to criticism, rejection, or misunderstanding, but when our confidence is rooted in Christ, we can face those challenges with courage.

One of the hardest parts of living boldly for Christ is dealing with the fear of rejection. Just like someone with a noticeable birthmark might fear being judged or rejected based on their appearance, we might fear being judged or rejected for our faith. It's natural to want to be accepted and liked by others, and when we sense that our beliefs are causing distance or discomfort in our relationships, it can be tempting to pull back or compromise. But Jesus Himself experienced rejection, and He warned His followers that we would face it too. In John 15:18, Jesus said, " If the world hate you, ye know that it hated me before it hated you." This doesn't mean we should go out of our way to provoke rejection, but it does remind us that following Christ will sometimes put us at odds with the world. However, we can find comfort in knowing that we are not alone in this. Jesus walks with us, and our identity in Him gives us the strength to endure any rejection or judgment we may face.

True confidence, the kind that isn't shaken by what others think, comes from understanding who we are in Christ. The world might judge us based on outward appearances, achievements, or social status, but God sees our hearts. He knows us intimately and loves us unconditionally. In Christ, we are forgiven, redeemed, and made new. We are no longer defined by our past mistakes, our failures, or the labels that others might try to put on us. Our identity is secure in Jesus, and nothing can take that away. When we truly grasp this, it changes everything.

We no longer have to seek validation from the world or worry about whether we measure up to its standards. We can live freely, knowing that we are already accepted by the One whose opinion matters most.

Living confidently in Christ also means embracing the gifts and calling that God has placed on our lives. Just as birthmarks make people unique, God has given each of us unique gifts, talents, and opportunities to serve Him. Sometimes, we might feel insecure about the gifts we have, especially when we compare ourselves to others. We might think, "I'm not as talented as they are," or, "I don't have anything special to offer." But God created each of us with a purpose, and He has equipped us with exactly what we need to fulfill that purpose. When we stop comparing ourselves to others and start focusing on who God made us to be, we can walk in confidence, knowing that He has a plan for our lives. Ephesians 2:10 says, "For we are his workmanship, created in Christ Jesus unto good works, which God hath before ordained that we should walk in them." This verse reminds us that we are God's masterpiece, and He has specific things for each of us to do. Our worth and confidence come from being His creation, designed for a purpose that only we can fulfill.

It's important to remember that confidence in Christ doesn't mean arrogance or thinking we're better than others. True confidence is humble because it recognizes that everything we have comes from God. It's not about boasting in our own abilities or trying to prove ourselves to others. Instead, it's about trusting in God's strength and His love for us. Confidence in Christ is quiet but strong—it doesn't need the approval of others to feel secure. It's the kind of confidence that allows us to be kind, generous, and loving, even when the world is harsh or critical. It's the confidence that comes from knowing that no matter what happens, we are deeply loved by God and that His plans for us are good.

Sometimes, our confidence in Christ will be tested. Just as someone with a birthmark might have moments of insecurity, there will be times when we doubt ourselves or feel uncertain about our faith. We might face situations that challenge our beliefs or make us question whether we're strong enough to keep going. In those moments, it's important to go back to God's Word and remind ourselves of the truth. Galatians 3:26 tells us, "For ye are all the children of God by faith in Christ Jesus." This simple yet powerful truth is the foundation of our confidence. We are children of God, not because of anything we've done, but because of what Jesus has done for us. Our identity is not something we earn; it's a gift we receive through faith. When we hold on to this truth, we can face any challenge with courage, knowing that God is with us and that He will never leave us.

In conclusion, just as birthmarks can impact self-esteem, living boldly for Christ can sometimes bring challenges. But true confidence doesn't come from the approval of others or from trying to fit in with the world. It comes from knowing our identity in Christ. We are children of God, loved, forgiven, and chosen. This truth gives us the strength to live boldly for Him, even when it's hard. We don't have to fear rejection or judgment because we know that our worth is found in Jesus, not in the opinions of others. As we walk in confidence, rooted in our identity in Christ, we can embrace the unique calling that God has placed on our lives, knowing that He has a purpose for us. And even when we face challenges, we can trust that God is with us, guiding us, and strengthening us every step of the way. So let us live boldly for Christ, not afraid of what others might think, but secure in the knowledge that we are children of God, and that is where our true confidence comes from.

Conclusion

As we come to the end of "The Birthmark of the Believer", my hope is that you now feel a deeper sense of what it truly means to be marked by your faith in Christ. This journey isn't one that ends when you close this book. It's a lifelong walk of growing closer to God, becoming more like Jesus, and living out your faith boldly in a world that might not always understand or accept it. The birthmark of the believer is a sign of God's love, grace, and purpose written on your heart. It's a reminder that you belong to Him, that you've been set apart, and that you have a special role to play in His kingdom. As you move forward, remember that this birthmark is not just something you carry in private, but it's meant to be seen in how you live every day. Your actions, your words, your choices—they are all reflections of the faith that defines you. The world may push back, challenges may arise, and there will be times when your faith feels heavy, but you are not alone. God is with you, guiding you, strengthening you, and equipping you for every step of the journey ahead. Don't be discouraged when the path gets difficult. Remember, every trial is an opportunity for growth, for God to refine you and make you even more like Him. Stay rooted in His Word, seek His presence in prayer, and surround yourself with other believers who will encourage you and walk beside you. Keep your eyes on Jesus, the author and finisher of your faith, knowing that He will never leave you or forsake you. You are marked by His love, and nothing can take that away. As you continue to live out your faith, let the world see the difference that Christ has made in you. Be a light, shining brightly in the darkness, showing others the hope, peace, and joy that comes from knowing the Savior. This birthmark of faith is a beautiful gift, and it is one that will lead you through every season of life, from the highest highs to the deepest valleys. So, carry it proudly. Walk confidently in who you are in Christ, and trust that God has an amazing plan for your life. The journey may not always be easy, but it is full of purpose and promise. Keep pressing forward, living in the fullness of the identity you have in Jesus, knowing that the best is yet to come. You are His, and that is more than enough to carry you through every challenge and every triumph that lies ahead. Continue to walk boldly in your faith, remembering that your birthmark as a believer reflects the incredible love God has for you, and it is your invitation to live a life of true meaning and eternal significance.

Don't miss out!

Visit the website below and you can sign up to receive emails whenever Joshua Rhoades publishes a new book. There's no charge and no obligation.

https://books2read.com/r/B-A-AJLBB-ADKCF

BOOKS2READ

Connecting independent readers to independent writers.

Did you love *The Birthmark of the Believer*? Then you should read *Why Did Jesus Weep?*[1] by Joshua Rhoades!

[2]

In John 11, we witness one of the most emotional moments in Jesus' ministry—His weeping at the tomb of Lazarus. This act raises a profound question: Why Did Jesus Weep? Was it a mere reaction to the sorrow around Him, or was there a deeper meaning to His tears? This book looks into that very question, revealing Jesus' compassion and His divine response to human suffering. His tears were not just for Lazarus but for all of humanity, showing us that Jesus is intimately involved in our pain.

His weeping wasn't a fleeting response but a reflection of His deep empathy and love for a broken world. Through lessons like "Death's Devastation" and "The Desire for Restoration," this book uncovers how His tears mirror His heart for us, offering comfort in times of loss and struggle. Jesus' tears weren't a sign of weakness but a declaration of His divine purpose. Following His tears, He raised Lazarus from the dead, foreshadowing His own resurrection and triumph over sin and death.

---

1. https://books2read.com/u/bPnNEd

2. https://books2read.com/u/bPnNEd

For believers, the question Why Did Jesus Weep? is a call to trust in Jesus' power, love, and promises, even amidst suffering. His tears invite us to embrace His compassion and extend it to others, offering hope in a hurting world. This book reminds us that Jesus' weeping was not just an emotional moment but a message of hope and restoration for all who follow Him.